Alphabet Pictures

The alphabet can be fun, especially when you combine it with pictures that can be colored. Here are all the letters of the alphabet, along with pictures corresponding to words that begin with each letter. Learn how to spell the words and color in the pictures with crayons, colored pencils, paint or magic marker.

My First
ABC
Picture Coloring Book

Deb T. Bunnell

Dover Publications, Inc.
New York

Bibliographical Note

My First ABC Picture Coloring Book is a new work, first published by Dover Publications, Inc., in 1996.

DOVER *Pictorial Archive* SERIES

International Standard Book Number: 0-486-29143-X

Manufactured in the United States of America
Dover Publications, Inc., 31 East 2nd Street, Mineola, N.Y. 11501

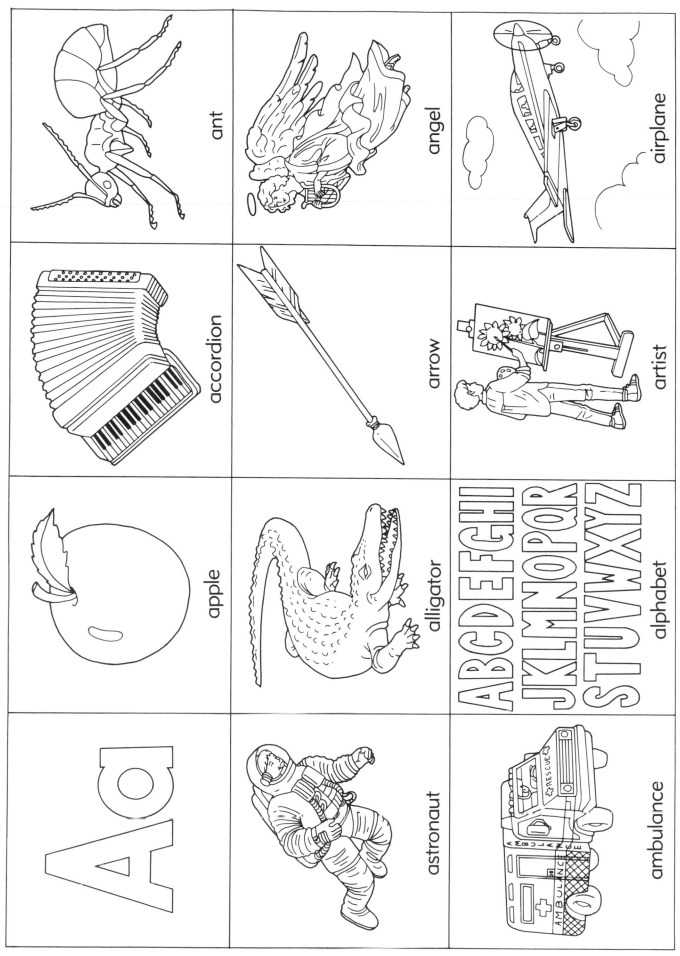

ant

angel

airplane

accordion

arrow

artist

apple

alligator

alphabet

Aa

astronaut

ambulance

1

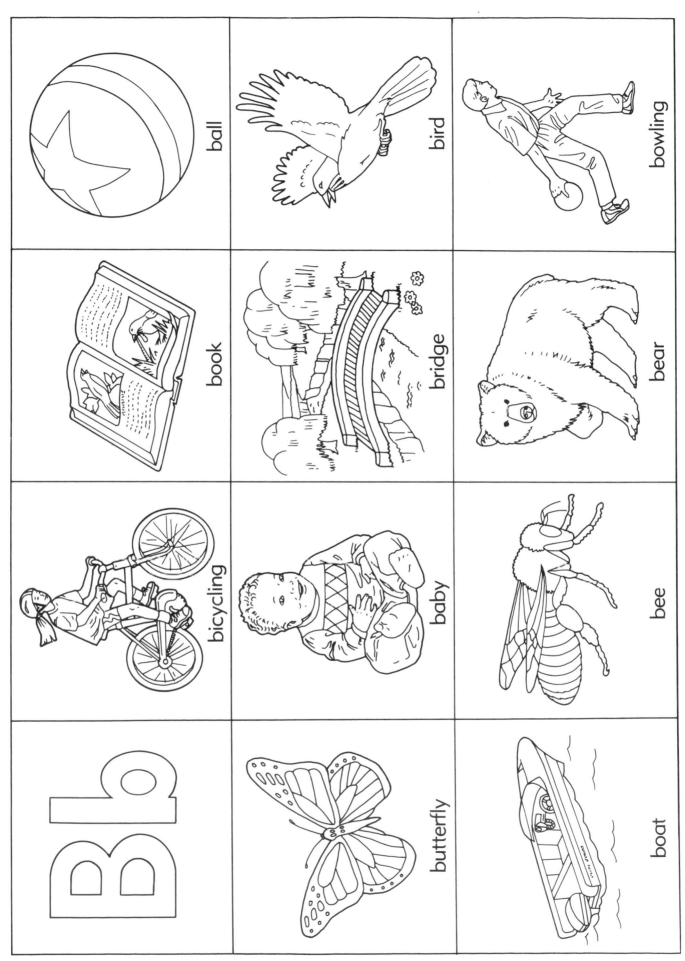

ball

bird

bowling

book

bridge

bear

bicycling

baby

bee

Bb

butterfly

boat

2

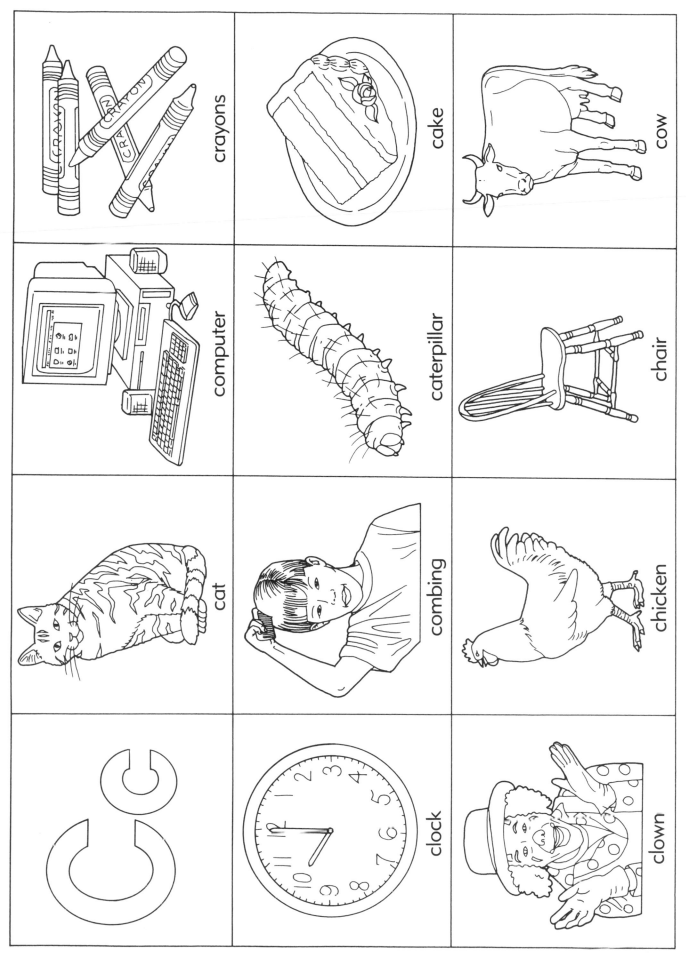

crayons

cake

cow

computer

caterpillar

chair

cat

combing

chicken

Cc

clock

clown

3

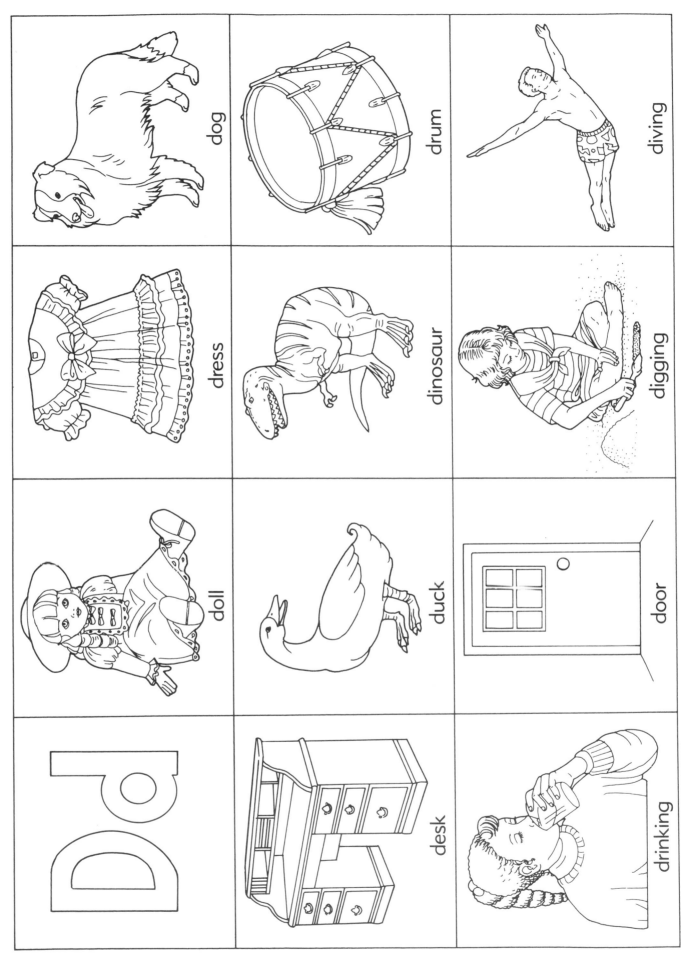

dog

drum

diving

dress

dinosaur

digging

doll

duck

door

Dd

desk

drinking

4

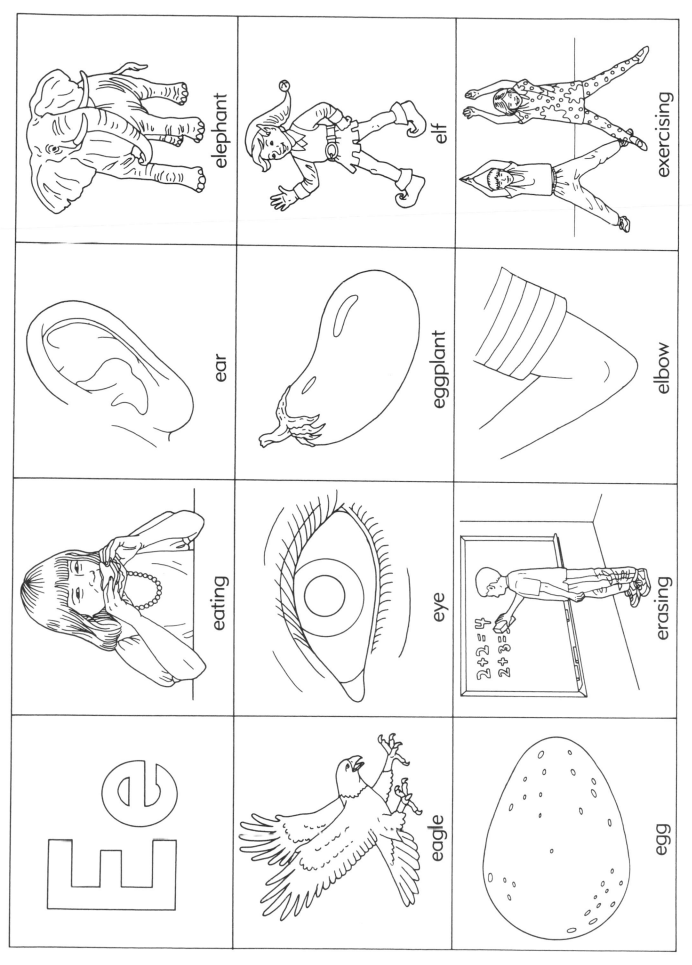

elephant

elf

exercising

ear

eggplant

elbow

eating

eye

erasing

Ee

eagle

egg

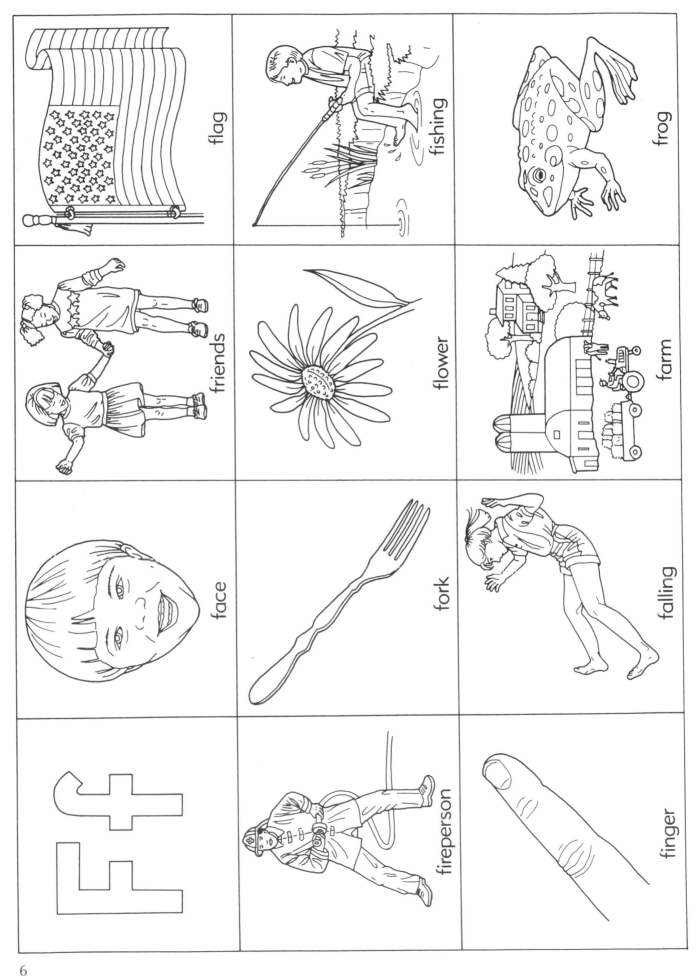

flag

fishing

frog

friends

flower

farm

face

fork

falling

Ff

fireperson

finger

goose

giraffe

gorilla

girl

ghost

golfing

grapes

goldfish

glasses

Gg

goat

guitar

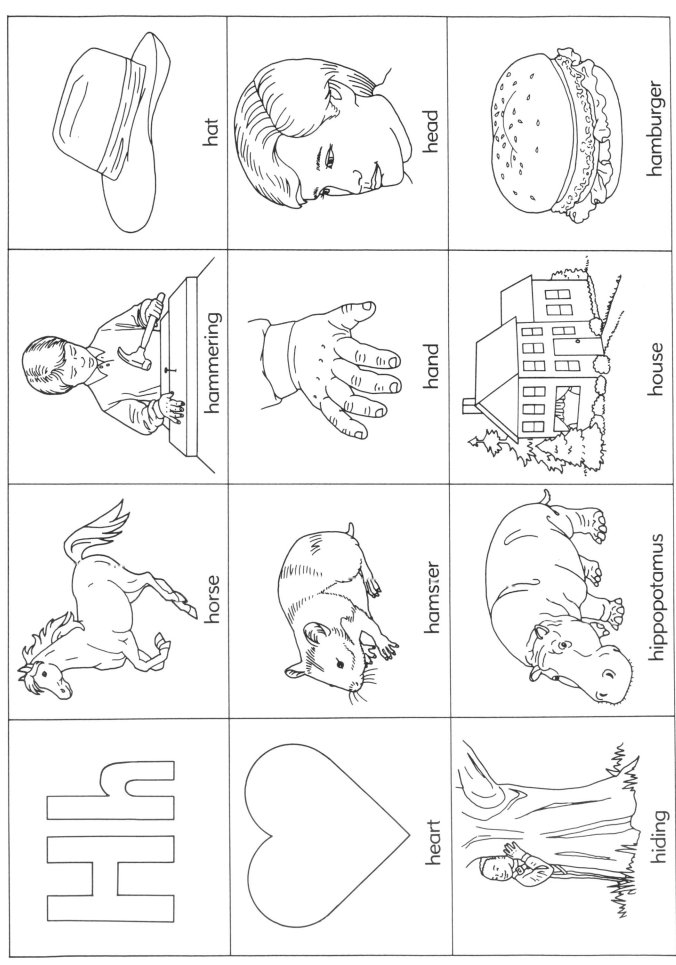

hat

head

hamburger

hammering

hand

house

horse

hamster

hippopotamus

Hh

heart

hiding

8

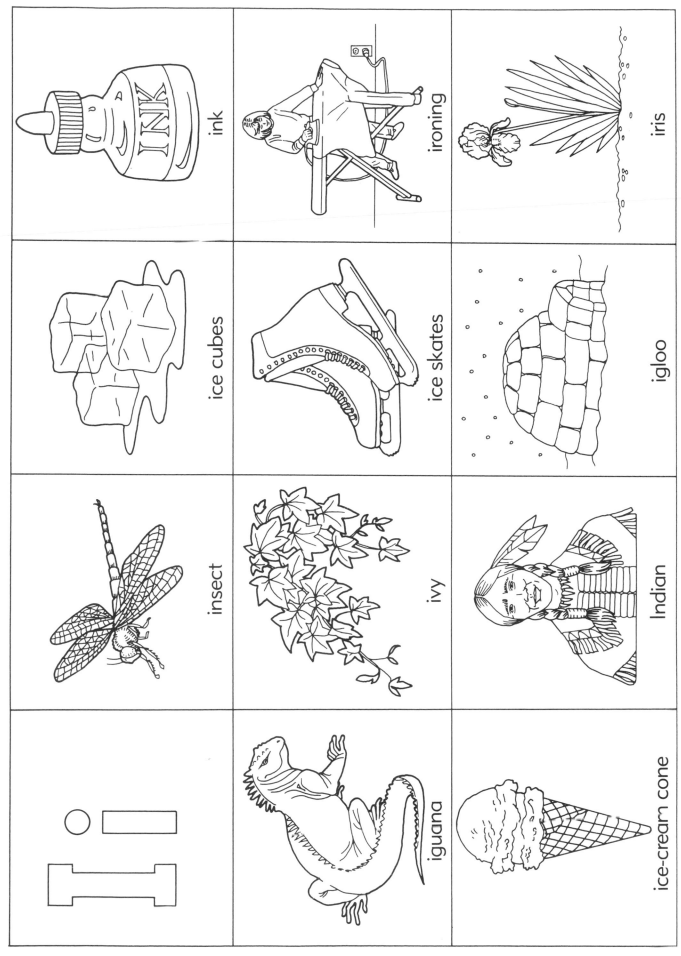

ink

ironing

iris

ice cubes

ice skates

igloo

insect

ivy

Indian

I i

iguana

ice-cream cone

9

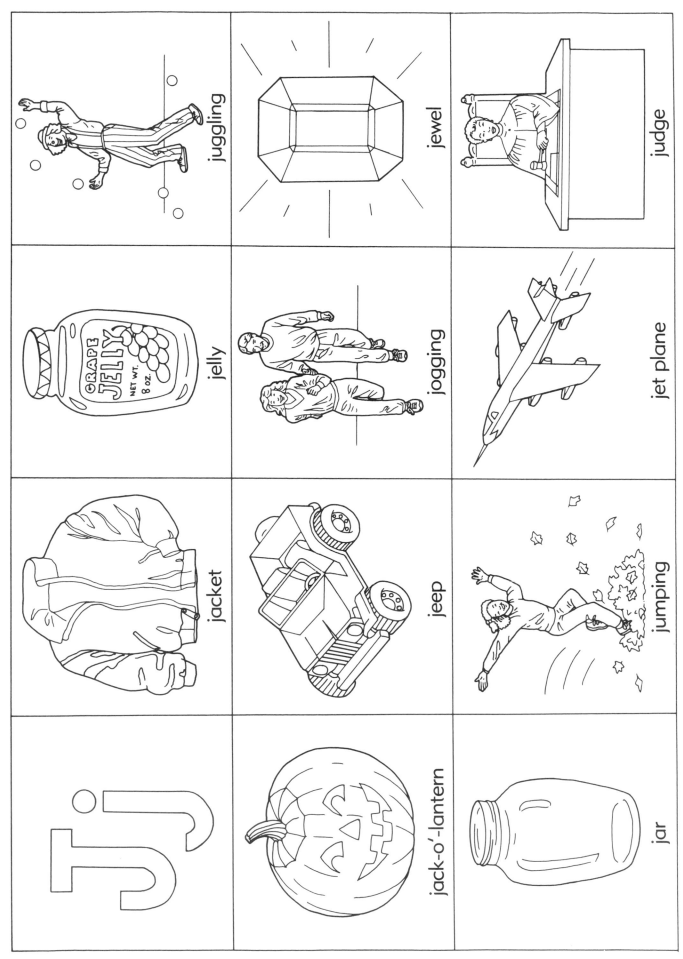

juggling

jewel

judge

jelly

jogging

jet plane

jacket

jeep

jumping

jack-o'-lantern

jar

10

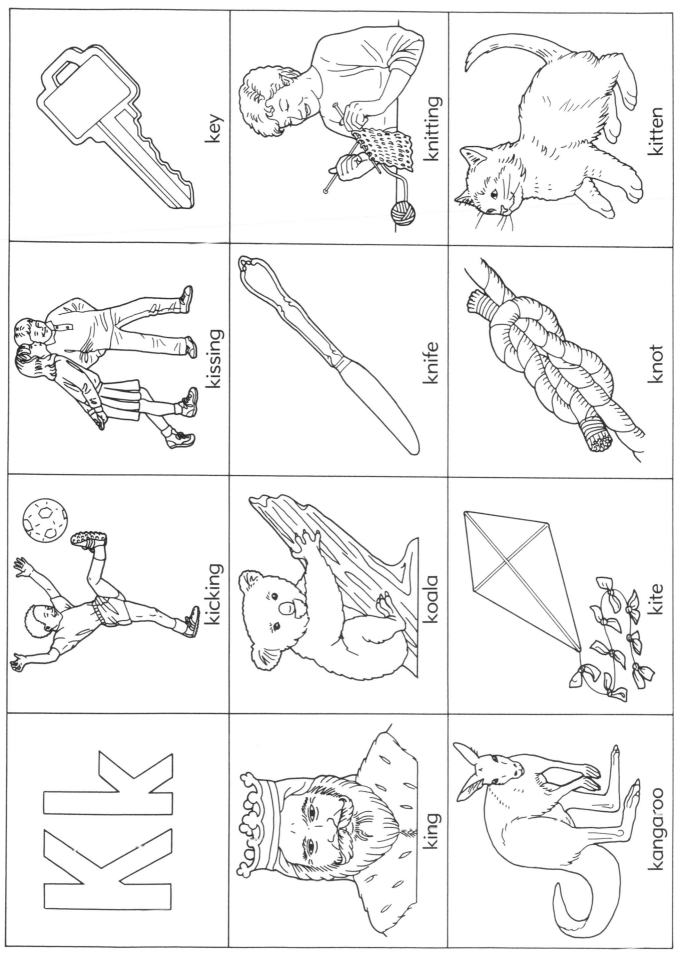

key

knitting

kitten

kissing

knife

knot

kicking

koala

kite

Kk

king

kangaroo

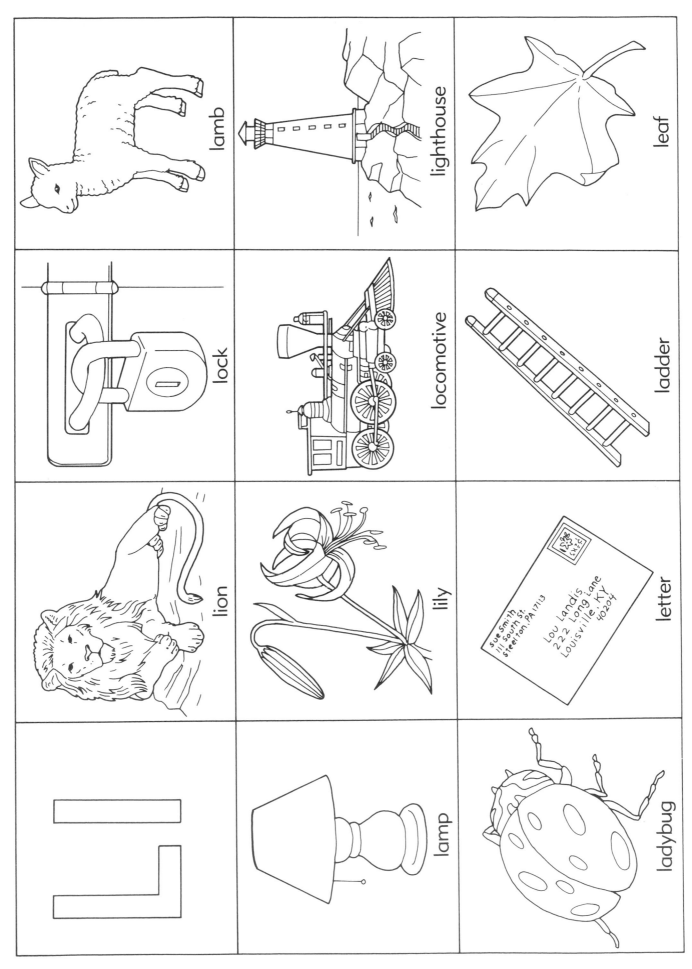

lamb

lighthouse

leaf

lock

locomotive

ladder

lion

lily

letter

L l

lamp

ladybug

12

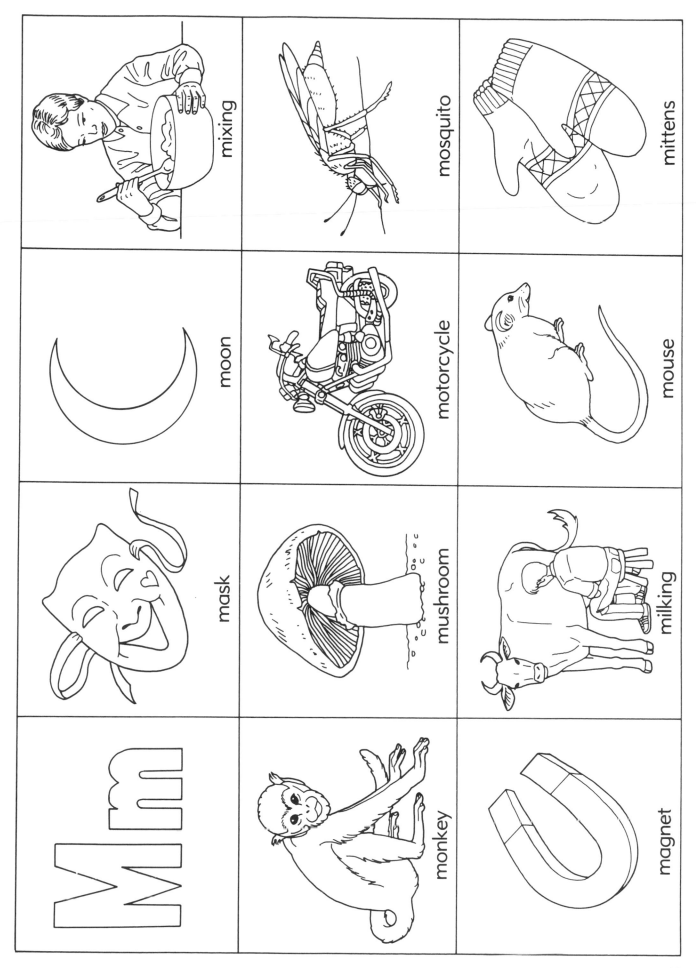

mixing

mosquito

mittens

moon

motorcycle

mouse

mask

mushroom

milking

Mm

monkey

magnet

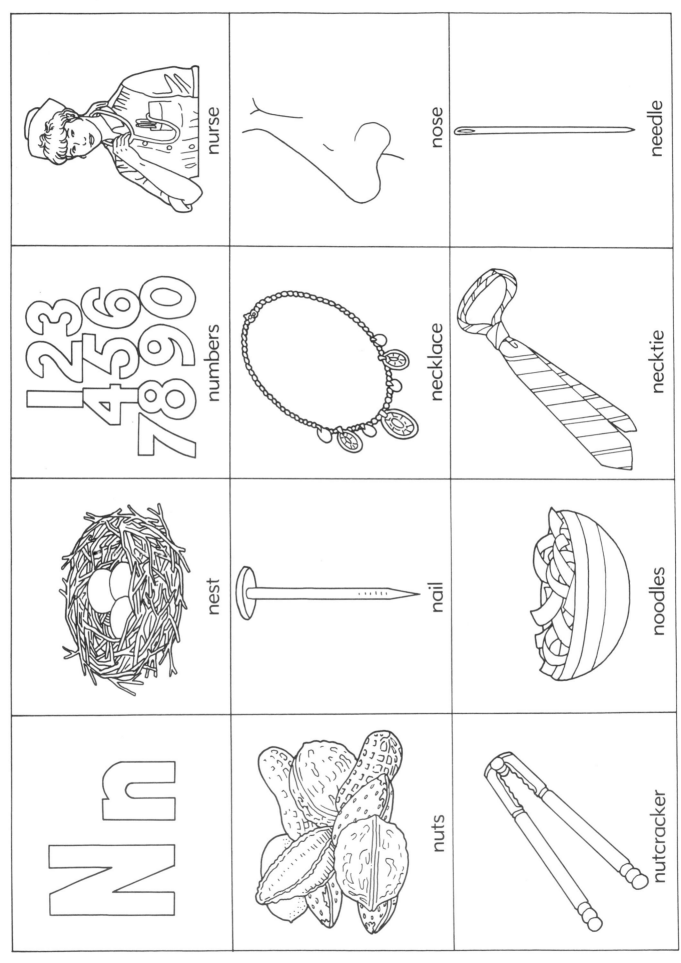

nurse

nose

needle

numbers

necklace

necktie

nest

nail

noodles

Nn

nuts

nutcracker

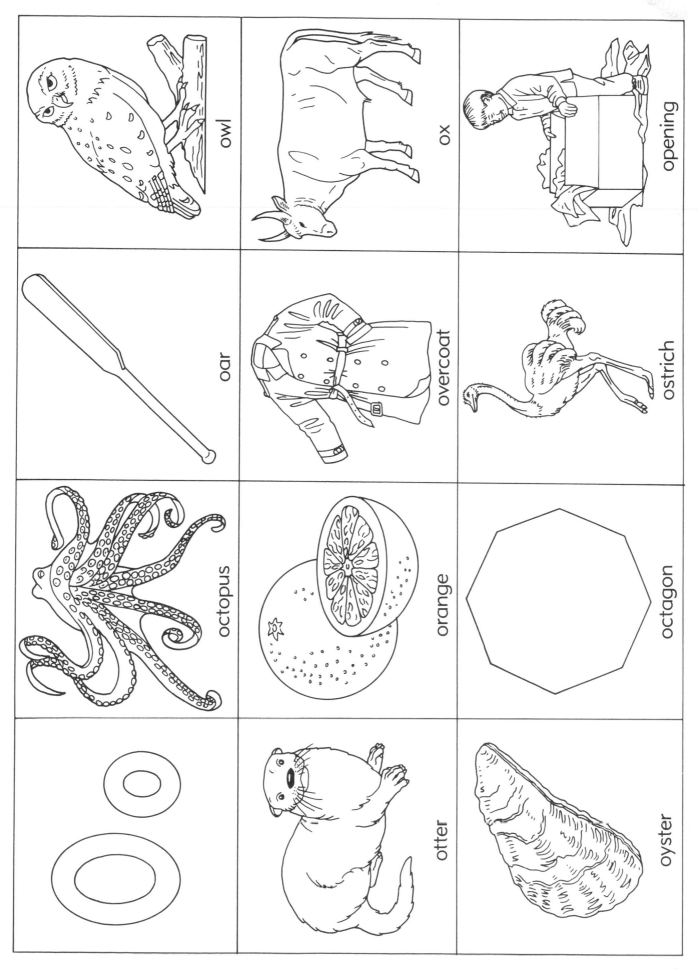

owl

ox

opening

oar

overcoat

ostrich

octopus

orange

octagon

otter

oyster

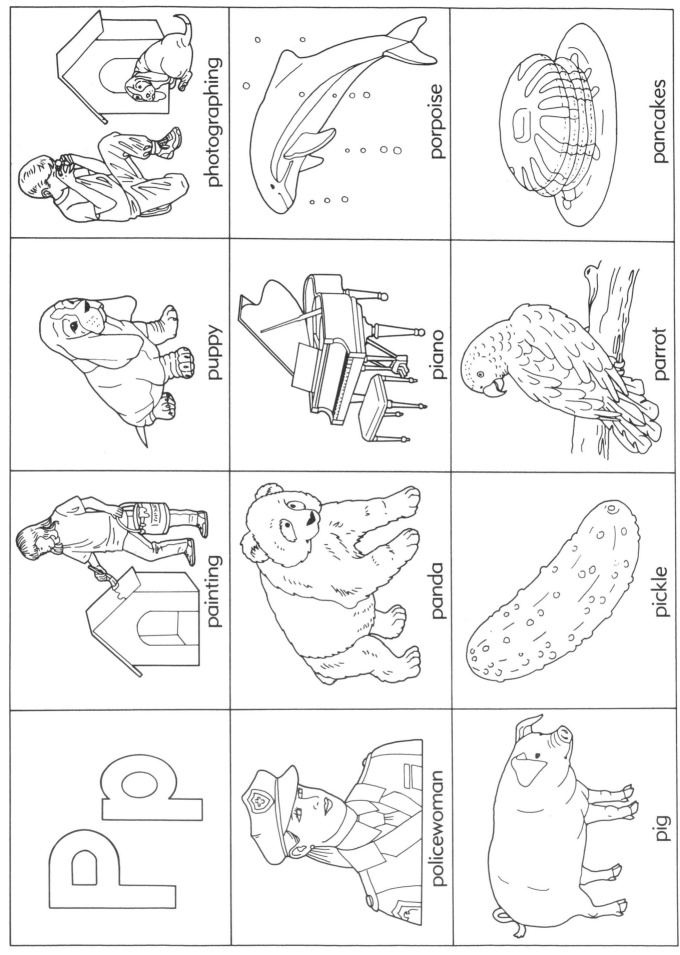

photographing

porpoise

pancakes

puppy

piano

parrot

painting

panda

pickle

Pp

policewoman

pig

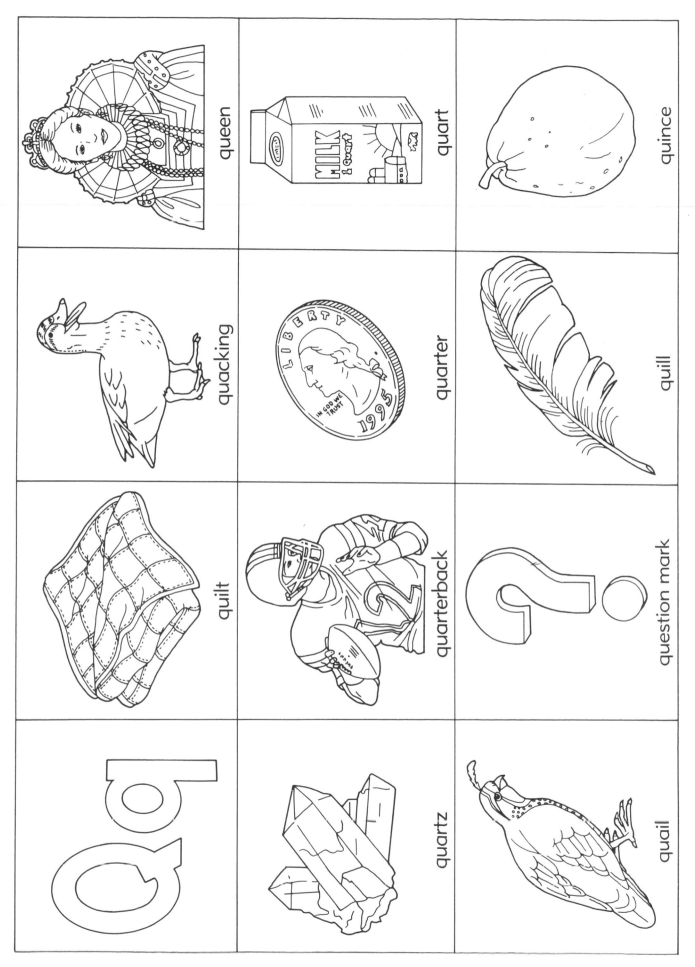

queen

quart

quince

quacking

quarter

quill

quilt

quarterback

question mark

Qq

quartz

quail

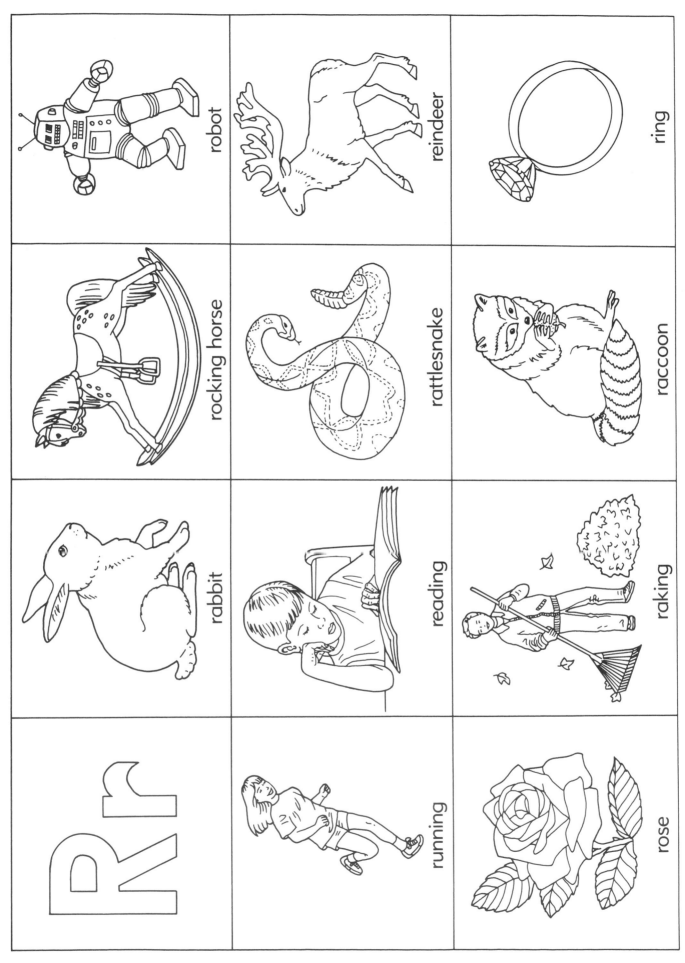

robot

reindeer

ring

rocking horse

rattlesnake

raccoon

rabbit

reading

raking

Rr

running

rose

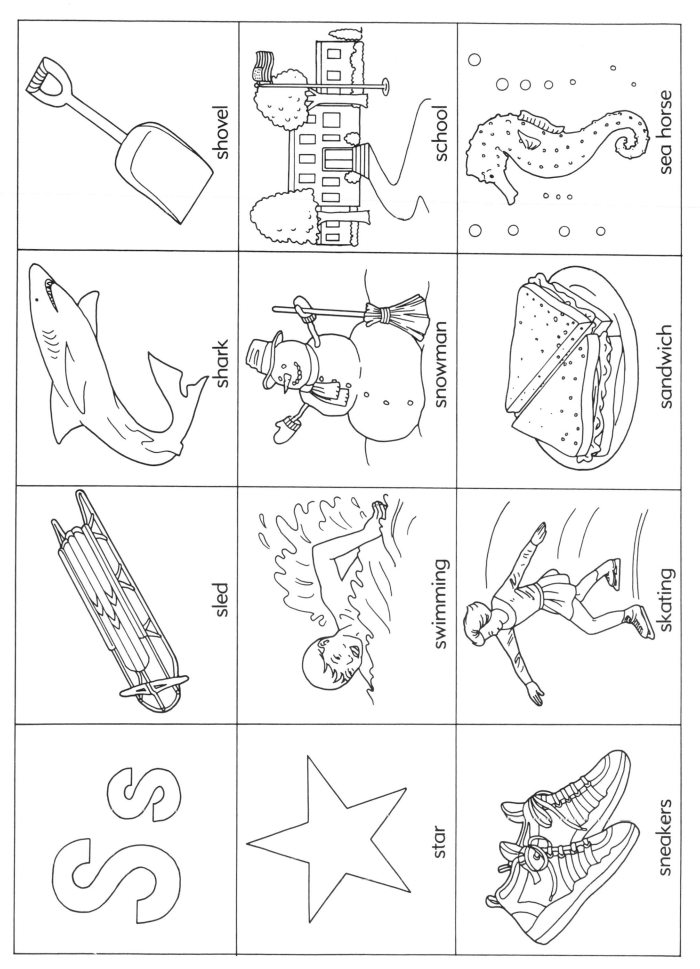

shovel

school

sea horse

shark

snowman

sandwich

sled

swimming

skating

Ss

star

sneakers

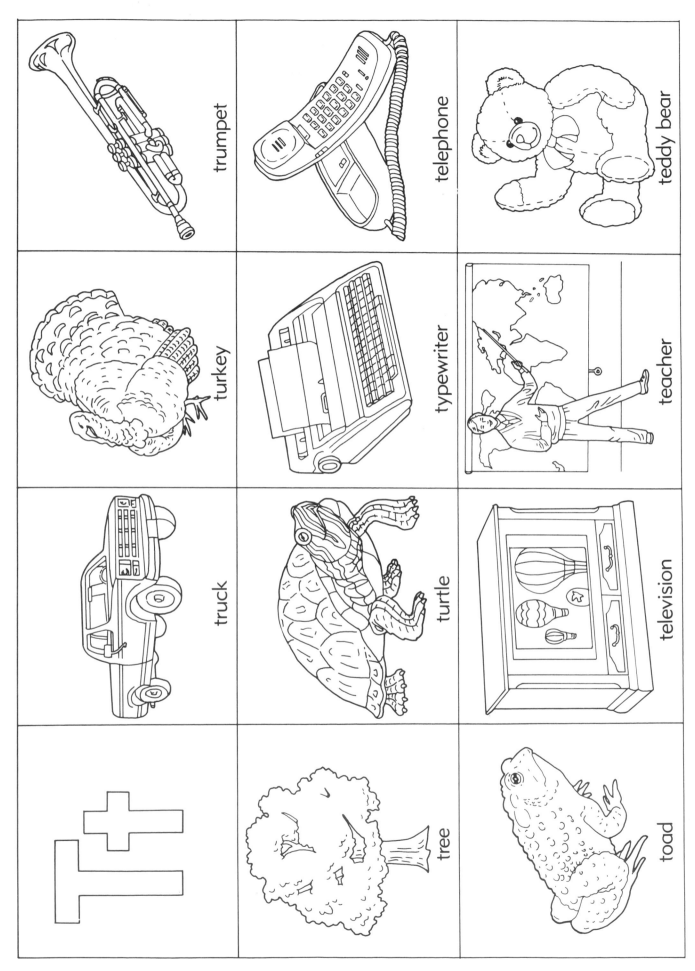

trumpet

telephone

teddy bear

turkey

typewriter

teacher

truck

turtle

television

Tt

tree

toad

20

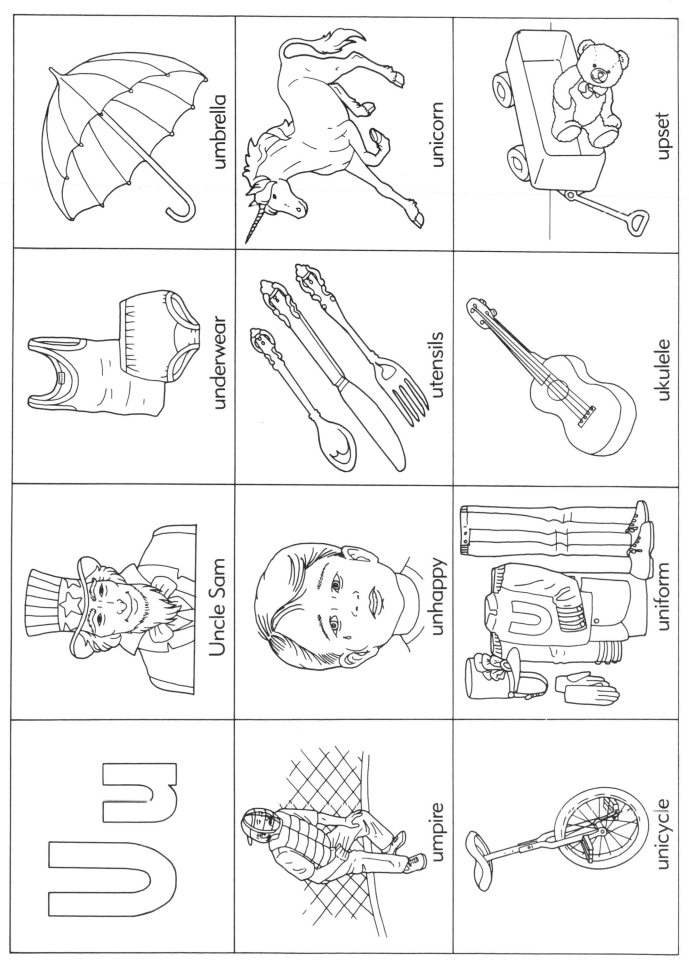

umbrella

unicorn

upset

underwear

utensils

ukulele

Uncle Sam

unhappy

uniform

Uu

umpire

unicycle

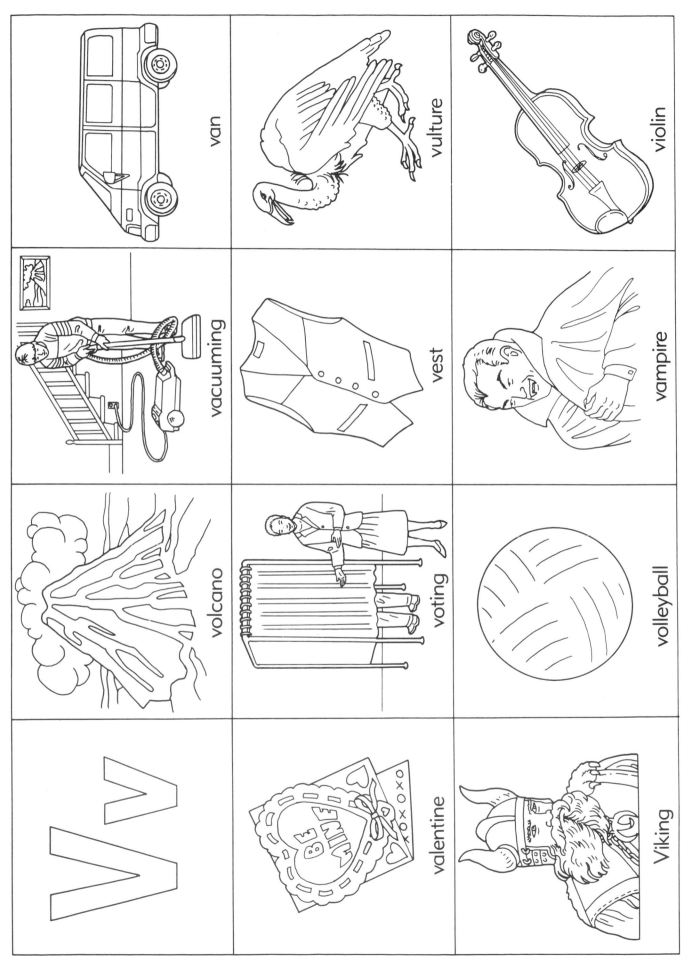

van

vulture

violin

vacuuming

vest

vampire

volcano

voting

volleyball

Vv

valentine

Viking

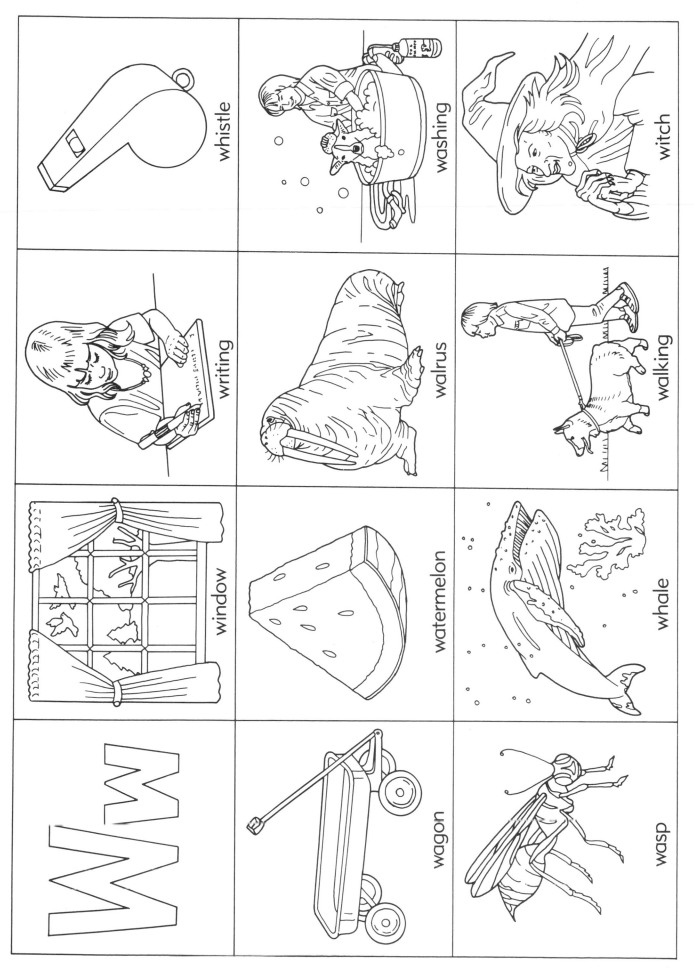

whistle

washing

witch

writing

walrus

walking

window

watermelon

whale

W/w

wagon

wasp

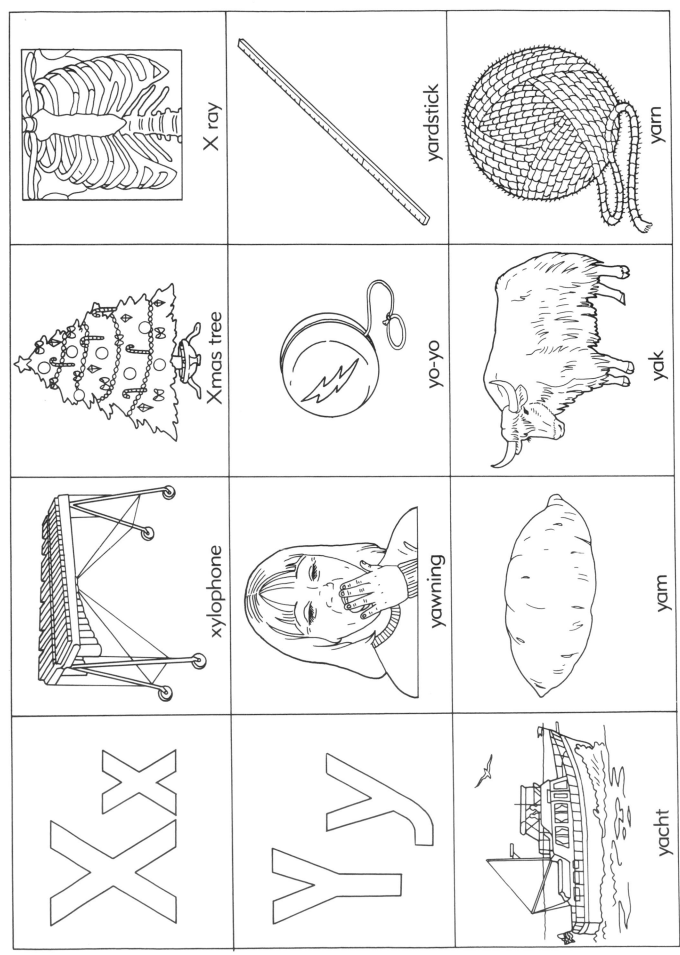

X ray

yardstick

yarn

Xmas tree

yo-yo

yak

xylophone

yawning

yam

X x

Y y

yacht

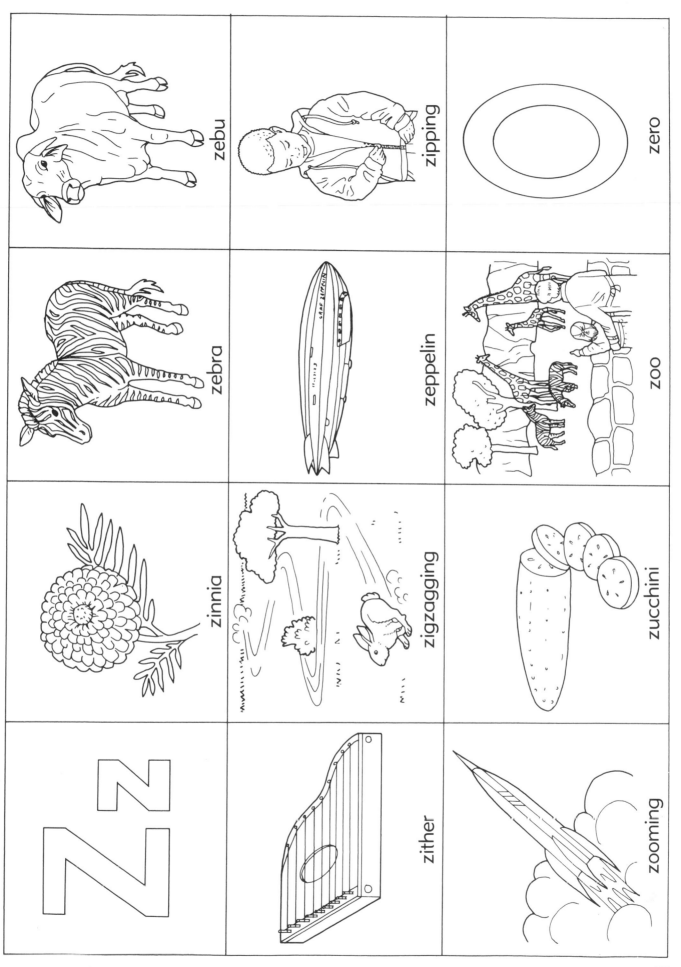

zebu

zipping

zero

zebra

zeppelin

zoo

zinnia

zigzagging

zucchini

Zz

zither

zooming